W9-ATG-360

GALLUP GUIDES FOR YOUTH FACING PERSISTENT PREJUDICE

Hispanics

GALLUP GUIDES FOR YOUTH FACING PERSISTENT PREJUDICE

- Asians
- Blacks
- Hispanics
- Jews
- The LGBT Community
- Muslims
- Native North American Indians
- People with Mental and Physical Challenges

GALLUP GUIDES FOR YOUTH FACING PERSISTENT PREJUDICE

Hispanics

Ellyn Sanna

Mason Crest

Mason Crest
370 Reed Road
Broomall, Pennsylvania 19008
www.masoncrest.com

Printed and bound in the United States of America.

First printing
9 8 7 6 5 4 3 2 1

ISBN-13: 978-1-4222-2462-5 (hardcover series)
ISBN-13: 978-1-4222-2465-6 (hardcover)
ISBN-13: 978-1-4222-9338-6 (e-book)

Cataloging-in-Publication Data on file with Library of Congress.

Seba, Jaime.
 Gallup guides for youth facing persistent prejudice. Hispanics / by Jaime Seba.
     p. cm.
 Includes bibliographical references and index.
 ISBN 978-1-4222-2465-6 (hardcover) -- ISBN 978-1-4222-2462-5 (series hardcover) -- ISBN 978-1-4222-9338-6 (ebook)
 1. Hispanic Americans--Juvenile literature. 2. Prejudices--Juvenile literature. 3. Racism--Juvenile literature. I. Title. II. Title: Hispanics.
 E184.S75S43 2013
 305.86'8073--dc23
                                       2012019562

Produced by Harding House Publishing Services, Inc.
www.hardinghousepages.com
Interior design by Micaela Sanna.
Page design elements by Cienpies Design / Illustrations | Dreamstime.com.
Cover design by Torque Advertising + Design.

Thank you to Pastor Angel Campos at Monte Visto Church and Nicole González Patterson and Sal Rivera at the Arizona Latino Research Enterprise and the Rivera Law Group, P.C., for their generous help in the creation of this book. Thanks also to Lauren Wilsey for her photography.

CONTENTS

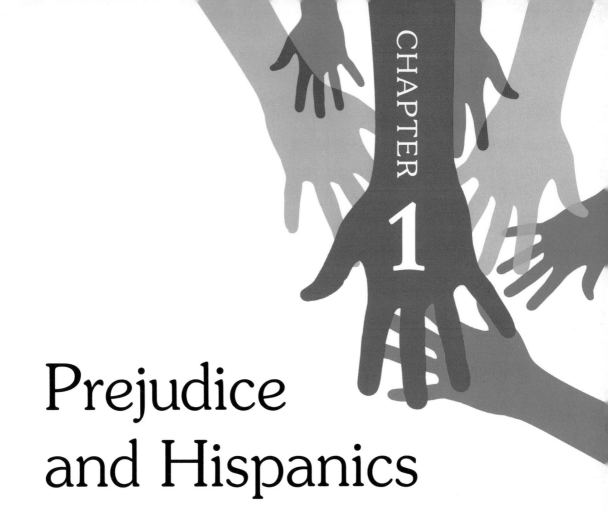

Prejudice and Hispanics

Angel Campos was born in Mexico. Today he is an American citizen and a pastor in Phoenix, Arizona. He works every day with Hispanic immigrants—and he knows all too well the reality of prejudice.

"A lot of the time," he says, "people around here think they know who a Hispanic is, just by looking at him. They see someone with brown skin and black hair, someone who looks like they speak Spanish—and they think, *There's a gang member. There's an illegal immigrant. There's a drug dealer.*"

What Pastor Campos is describing is one of the thought patterns that give prejudice so much strength. It's called stereotyping.

STEREOTYPES

A stereotype is a fixed, commonly held idea or image of a person or group that's based on an **oversimplification** of some observed or imagined trait. Stereotypes assume that whatever is believed about a group is typical for each and every individual within that group. "All blondes are dumb,"

High School Stereotypes

The average high school has its share of stereotypes—lumping a certain kind of person together, ignoring all the ways that each person is unique. These stereotypes are often expressed with a single word or phrase: "jock," "nerd," "goth," "prep," or "geek." The images these words call to mind are easily recognized and understood by others. But that doesn't mean they're true!

Group Pressure

Why do people continue to believe stereotypes despite evidence that may not support them? Researchers have found that it may have something to do with group pressure. During one experiment, seven members of a group were asked to state that a short line is longer than a long line. About a third of the rest of the group agreed that the short line was longer, despite evidence to the contrary. Apparently, people conform to the beliefs of those around them in order to gain group acceptance.

is a stereotype. "Women are poor drivers," is another. "Men are slobs," is yet another, and "Gay men are **effeminate**," is one as well.

Many stereotypes tend to make us feel superior in some way to the person or group being stereotyped. Not all stereotypes are negative, however; some are positive—"Black men are good at basketball," "Gay guys have good fashion sense," or "Asian students are smart"—but that still doesn't make them true. Even positive stereotypes ignore individuals' uniqueness. They make assumptions that may or may not be accurate.

We can't help our human tendency to put people into categories. As babies, we faced a confusing world filled with an amazing variety of new things. We needed a way to make sense of it all, so one of our first steps in learning about the world around us was to sort things into separate slots in our heads: small furry things that said *meow* were kitties, while larger furry things that said *arf-arf* were doggies; cars went *vroom-vroom*, but trains were longer and went *choo-choo*;

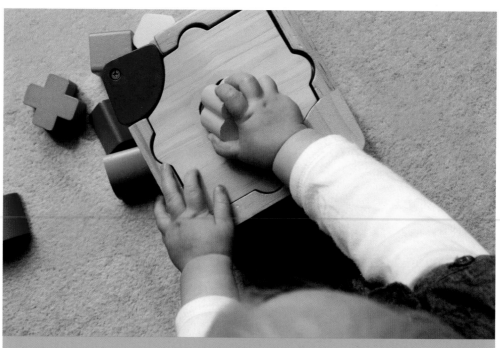

Learning to notice and sort differences is an important developmental skill that babies learn.

little girls looked one way and little boys another; and doctors wore white coats, while police officers wore blue. These were our earliest stereotypes. They were a handy way to make sense of the world; they helped us know what to expect, so that each time we faced a new person or thing, we weren't starting all over again from scratch.

But stereotypes become dangerous when we continue to hold onto our mental images despite new evidence. (For instance, as a child you may have decided that all dogs bite—which means that when faced by friendly, harmless dogs, you assume they're dangerous and so you miss out on getting to know all dogs.) Stereotypes are particularly dangerous and destructive when they're directed at persons or groups of persons. That's when they turn into prejudice.

WHAT IS PREJUDICE?

The root word of prejudice is "pre-judge." Prejudiced people often judge others based purely on their race or ethnic group; they make assumptions about others that may have no basis in reality. They believe that if your skin is darker or you speak a different language or wear different clothes or worship God in a different way, then they already know you are not as smart, not as nice, not as honest, not as valuable, or not as moral as they are. Hispanics have been the victims of prejudice for hundreds of years.

Why do human beings experience prejudice? **Sociologists** believe humans have a basic tendency to fear anything that's unfamiliar or unknown. Someone who is strange (in that they're not like us) is scary; they're automatically dangerous or inferior. If we get to know the strangers, of course, we end up discovering that they're not so different from ourselves. They're not so frightening and threatening after all. But too often, we don't let that happen. We put up a wall between the strangers and ourselves. We're on the inside; they're on the outside. And then we peer over the wall, too far away from the people on the other side to see anything but our differences.

RACISM

Prejudice and racism go hand-in-hand. Prejudice is an attitude, a way of looking at the world. When it turns into action it's called discrimination. Discrimination is when people are treated differently (and unfairly) because they belong to a particular group of people. Racism is a combination of the two. It's treating members of a certain "race" differently because you think they're not as good, simply because they belong to that race. You might say that prejudice is the root of racism—and discrimination is its branches and leaves.

There's one other concept that's important to racism as well—the belief that human beings can be divided into groups that are truly separate and different from one another.

The concept of race divides human beings into groups. Scientists are not convinced that this is an accurate way of looking at the world, since all human beings are biologically more alike than they are different.

Hispanic or Latino?

In the 1980s, the U.S. government came up with the name "Hispanic" for people who speak Spanish and live in the United States. Not everyone likes this name. Many people don't like the way the term lumps everyone together based only on language. The people in North and South America who speak Spanish have a very different culture from Spain's. Other people use the word "Latino" for this same group of people. They like this word better because it has more to do with Latin America than with Spain.

The fact that Hispanics—or Latinos—don't agree on which term to use for themselves shows how different they all are. They come from many different countries. They have different stories. But at the same time, Hispanic American cultures have many things in common. They share many of the same stories. They often worship God the same way. Many of the same things are important to them. They are proud of their art and music. They celebrate the same holidays.

Scientists aren't convinced this is really possible, though. Biologically, people are more alike than they're different, no matter what color their skin is or what continent their ancestors came from.

Hispanics are just as likely to be smart as Anglos (people whose ancestors came from England or other parts of Europe). Latinos are just as trustworthy and kind, just as moral and hardworking. Some Hispanics get in trouble with the law—and so do some Anglos. Many Latinos have problems. So do many Anglos.

Racism tells lies. Prejudice is one of those lies.

TELLING THE TRUTH

Nicole González Patterson is working hard to fight prejudice. She's a lawyer who also assisted with the Arizona Latino Research Center, an organization that was founded in 2004 by a group of Hispanic Americans, including Sal Rivera. Like Nicole, Sal is a lawyer. Nicole's background is Puerto Rican; Sal's is Mexican. Nicole's family speaks Spanish in the home; Sal was born in the United States and doesn't even speak Spanish well. And yet Sal is instantly indentified as Hispanic, while Nicole isn't. As a result, she hears racial slurs expressed around her, because people assume she's Anglo. "For me,

Nicole González Patterson is doing her part to counteract prejudice with education and communication.

Prejudice? Or Patriotism?

The Arizona state government passed a law in 2010 that put an end to ethnic studies in Arizona public schools, from kindergarten through twelfth grade. This meant that students in Arizona, where nearly one-third of the population is Latino, could no longer learn about Hispanic culture and history as part of their education. If districts are found in violation of the new law, the Arizona Department of Education can withhold 10 percent of a district's state funding.

Many teachers, parents, and students said the law was motivated purely by prejudice. People around the world felt the law was a good example of refusing to allow the truth to be told. Meanwhile, the state government justified the law by saying that Hispanic studies encourage resentment toward a race or class of people (in other words, they encourage Latinos to resent Anglos), they are designed primarily for pupils of one ethnic group, and they promote ethnic solidarity. The government leaders who backed the law also insisted that ethnic studies could eventually encourage the overthrow of the U.S. government. They claimed they were motivated by patriotism, not prejudice.

We keep our prejudices intact when we refuse to look at the truth.

personally" says Nicole, "prejudice is subtle. It's what makes me uncomfortable speaking Spanish in public."

One of the goals of the Arizona Latino Research Center is to "represent and personalize the face and soul of many Latinos who are frequently and popularly treated as nameless members of our society." Nicole and her colleagues are speaking the truth in the face of prejudice's lies.

Four Characteristics of Prejudice

1. a feeling of superiority
2. a feeling that the minority is different and alien
3. a feeling of rightful claim to power, privilege, and status
4. a fear and suspicion that the minority wants to take the power, privilege, and status from the dominant group

Truth can be a tricky thing. People can use only pieces of the truth. They can twist those pieces that don't fit their stereotypes and prejudices. They can refuse to see truths that make them uncomfortable.

People who are prejudiced aren't evil. We all have prejudices. But we can choose not to act on our prejudices. We can also choose to fight the prejudice inside our own minds by being open to the whole truth.

Hispanic History

One way to fight prejudice is to learn about another group's history. By finding out the events that shaped a group of people, we can learn to understand them better. Latinos have a long and proud history that's full of color and adventure, as well as tragedy and hardship.

TWO WORLDS MEET

In October 1492, two groups of people met on a beach in the Bahamas. It was one of the most important meetings in the whole history of the world.

On the east side of the Atlantic Ocean is the continent of Europe. By 1492, the people of Europe had become very interested in exploring the world. Now they looked at the great Atlantic Ocean and wondered what was on the other side. Some Europeans thought that crossing the Atlantic Ocean might be a shortcut to Asia.

Across the Atlantic Ocean from Europe are the continents of North and South America, the Americas. Millions of people lived there in the fifteenth century. There were hundreds of different tribes and communities and kingdoms. Before 1492, no one in Europe knew about these lands and people. And the Native people of the Americas knew nothing about Europe until that first meeting on the beach. That day, when the Natives first met the Spanish, two worlds came together. The story of that meeting was the first story in the history of a new people. There would be many, many more stories to come.

The English built colonies to the east and north of North America, while the Spanish built settlements in Mexico, Central America, and South America. Things went a little differently in the Spanish colonies than they did in the English colonies. Many of the Spaniards earned a reputation for cold-hearted cruelty—and yet they did not completely wipe out entire civilizations the way the English did. Instead, the

This mural by Diego Rivera portrays the early interactions between the Spanish and Native people.

Spanish readily adopted whatever elements of Native society were **compatible** with their own, leaving the basic culture in place.

What's more, many Spanish men turned to Native women as their mates. Although they certainly had their share of prejudices, the Spanish, unlike the English, were accustomed to a society where dark-skinned people (the Islamic Moors, originally from Africa) mixed freely with those with lighter skin. As a result, not as much **stigma** was attached to intermarriage.

Many Spanish people came to New Spain between 1500 and 1700. First they came as explorers and conquerors. Later, whole families came to start new lives in the New World. They built houses and farms. They brought cows and pigs and sheep with them. They planted European crops like wheat and grapes. They built towns with big churches in the middle of them. Huge farms and cattle ranches spread across the land.

This street mural symbolizes the Latino story, the history of the new people who were born from the mix of Spanish and Native.

Parts of the New World began to look a lot like Spain. New Spain was becoming more and more Spanish.

But the Native people also had a lot to teach the settlers. They taught the settlers how to grow new crops. Corn, beans, squash, and chili peppers had been grown in Mexico for thousands of years. The first Spanish had never seen these plants. In South America, the Incas grew many different kinds of potatoes. This was a new food for the Spanish, too. So were tomatoes! All these crops were brought back to Europe.

Native people and Spanish people got to know each other better. They worshipped the same Christian God together. They spoke Spanish together. They shared what they knew about the world with each other. Spanish people and Native people continued to marry each other. They had families together. Slaves brought from Africa added to the mix. These new families mixed Spanish, Native, and sometimes African ways of doing things. Their culture was a new mixture of cultures. The music they made, the houses they lived in, and the food they ate all came from this blend of cultures.

After many years, many people in Mexico, Central America, and South America stopped thinking of themselves as either Spanish or Native. They really were a new people!

Meanwhile, the land of Mexico reached far north of its modern-day borders. Much of what is today America's Southwest used to be part of Mexico. Eventually, by the nineteenth century, the leader of this land was a young mixed-blood officer named Antonio López de Santa Anna.

ONGOING CONFLICT

Santa Anna's original goal was to rid the country of all pureblood Spaniards. He felt they had been in control way too long, and it was time for Mexico's own people to be in charge. As Santa Anna's ambition grew, he began seizing more and more power. He appointed himself president and was in and out of office eleven times between 1833 and 1855.

Meanwhile, as settlers from the United States began moving into northern Mexico, they talked of establishing their own country, independent of Mexico. By 1834, the Americans outnumbered the Mexicans in the northern part of Mexico. In 1835, these settlers declared their independence.

But Santa Anna was never one to give in without a fight. He attacked the Americans at the Alamo, defeating them soundly. At a later battle in San Jacinto, however, the Americans defeated the Mexicans and captured Santa Anna. Santa Anna

Oil painting of Antonio López de Santa Anna.

This map shows all the territory that was once part of Mexico (or New Spain). Much of what is now the United States was then Mexico—which means that Hispanics who lived in this part of the continent suddenly found themselves being considered foreigners in their own land when the United States gained possession of this territory.

was forced to sign the Velasco Agreement in 1836, giving northern Mexico its freedom.

Mexico, furious over this loss, **exiled** Santa Anna and refused to recognize the Velasco Agreement. For nine years, this area in northern Mexico was in **limbo**. It considered itself a free state, but Mexico still considered it part of the country. Finally, the United States admitted the land into the Union, and it became the state of Texas.

In response, Mexico declared war on the United States. The Mexican government **reconciled** with Santa Anna, and asked him to lead the war against the United States. The United States troops, led by General Zachary Taylor, were better prepared for battle than the Mexicans, and American forces captured Mexico City on September 14, 1847; the Mexican American war was officially over on February 2, 1848, when the Treaty of Guadalupe Hidalgo was signed. This treaty called for Mexico to turn over all land north of the Rio Grande River (Texas), as well as all the land from the Gila River to the Pacific Ocean (what is now California, Nevada, Utah, and Arizona, as well as parts of Wyoming, Colorado, and New Mexico).

Despite Santa Anna's military failures, Mexico allowed him to name himself dictator of Mexico. In order to raise funds for the military, he sold additional land to the United States—a piece of Mexico along the Gila River (present-day Arizona and New Mexico). This deal, called the Gadsden Purchase, was the last major change of Mexican boundary lines. Mexico had lost over 50 percent of its territory to the United States in just a few short years.

Whether they now lived in the United States or south of the new boundary lines, the years that followed were hard ones for the Mexican people. North of the border, in the United States, Mexicans now found themselves considered aliens even on their own lands. They faced both prejudice and poverty in the homeland that had once been their own.

A History of Migration

By the twenty-first century, American jobs paid about eight times as much as those in Mexico. This served as a powerful lure to Mexico's poverty-stricken people, and many Mexicans flooded across the border (both legally and illegally) to find jobs on America's farms and in its factories. "So long as a worker in Mexico earns $5 per day and a worker in the United States earns $60, immigration problems will continue," former Mexican President Vincente Fox said soon after he was elected.

The flow of immigrants looking for work across the border is not a new **phenomenon**. Today's numbers may be higher than ever before, but for the past century, Mexican Americans have been a major part of the American workforce.

During the World Wars, the American government's Bracero Program brought thousands of Mexicans into the United States as temporary workers to replace the American employees who had gone to war. However, these workers were not authorized to stay in the country, and many were mistreated and paid extremely low wages.

Despite this, many of the Braceros did not return to Mexico. The U.S. and Mexican governments realized that the "temporary" admission of workers into the United States had not worked out the way it was intended. Many farmers became dependent on the inexpensive migrant workers and stopped trying to fill positions on their farms with more expensive local workers—and despite the low pay, workers and their families became dependent on the income provided by the farmers. Their wages were often so low, however, that some people compared the program to government-approved slavery. Faced with such problems, the program was ended in 1964.

But the flood of workers from Mexico did not ebb. Between 1945 and 1955, some 7.5 million acres of new farmland had gone into production in America's western states—and the landowners needed workers. Smuggling **undocumented** workers into the United States became a well-paying business.

Today, anti-immigration feelings are strong in many areas of the United States. Most Americans forget that many Mexicans called the Southwest their homes long before the white-skinned Europeans came along. Unfortunately, prejudice is alive and well in the United States.

Despite this, young people, especially young men, continue to head north across the border from Mexico. Some of them came from still further south, from other Central American and South American countries. If they are caught and sent back, they will try again. In the United States they face prejudice—but they are strong and eager to work. It doesn't look like one of the greatest global migrations of modern times will end any time soon.

The economies of the United States and Mexico are tangled together. Unsnarling the situation has proved to be too difficult for either government. Businesses in the United States depend on Hispanic workers who are willing to take

Hispanics who cross the U.S. border illegally often face dangerous situations.

This neighborhood on the edge of Phoenix has many empty houses. Latino immigrants might be able to build up the community if they were allowed to become legal residents.

Coyotes

People who make their living smuggling Mexicans into the United States are called coyotes. Many of these individuals have organized systems that may include fleets of trucks or buses, secret hideouts, counterfeit documents for the workers, and guides that lead undocumented Mexicans across the border through treacherous land. Some coyotes are unscrupulous, and busloads of undocumented immigrants have been found dead, suffocated in crowded vehicles that lack adequate ventilation and cooling.

the lowest paying jobs, positions that few Anglo-Americans will accept.

Many American citizens resent these workers who come across the border. Americans fear that undocumented workers will take jobs away from Americans during a time when there are already not enough jobs to go around.

Economics is a complicated subject, but most experts agree that Hispanic workers actually have a positive effect on the American economy. Americans' resentment probably has more to do with prejudice than with actual economic hardships.

Pastor Angel Campos is very familiar with this reality. So is Nicole González Patterson. "There are streets full of empty houses in Phoenix," Pastor Campos points out. "Meanwhile, I have people in my church who could buy the houses. They have savings, they work hard, they want to a build a home and make a strong community. They would pay property taxes and help the city grow. But they can't. They're illegal. And no one wants to let them become citizens."

Undocumented Aliens

No one knows exactly how many undocumented aliens are in the United States. During the 1990s, experts guessed that there were probably somewhere between one and two million—and between 55 and 65 percent of these are Mexicans. They make up nearly 10 percent of America's population of Mexican descent.

In the 1950s up through the 1980s, most of these undocumented aliens found work as farm workers, but today that situation has changed. Today, more and more skilled workers from Mexican cities are seeking industrial and urban jobs. Many undocumented Mexicans work in hotels, restaurants, car washes, and health-care centers.

Mexican Wages

Minus benefits, take-home pay in Mexico averages $5 *per day*. That's less than the U.S. minimum *hourly* wage.

Nicole sees another side of this same problem. "In Arizona, many businesses depend on Latino workers," she says. "These business get raided by the police. If they're employing illegal workers, they're shut down. Obviously, shutting down businesses is horrible for the economy. It's bad for everyone. But not everyone sees that. They say, 'Latinos are a threat to our jobs,' and they don't realize all the ways that Latinos contribute to the American economy."

Ironically, Americans have often stereotyped Hispanics as lazy. The image of the napping Mexican in a big sombrero beneath a cactus is one that most Americans have seen. The reality is far different, for much of America's industry has been built on the energy and determination of Hispanic workers.

Prejudice is a hard enemy to fight—but understanding is one of the strongest weapons against it. We learn to open our minds and hearts when we really listen to others' stories.

Real-Life Stories

Angel Campos was born in Esperanza, Sonora, in Mexico, but when he was a teenager, his father went across the border into the United States to find work. As soon as he could, he went back to get his family; they crossed the border with visas for visiting Disneyland—and they never went back.

In the United States, the Campos had opportunities they didn't have in Mexico. The adults could get jobs; the children could go to school. The family had enough to eat.

Ignacio works at Pastor Campos' church. Like Pastor Campos, Ignacio does what he can to fight the effects of prejudice. When people he knows are deported, he brings food and clothing across the border to them.

As undocumented immigrants, however, they also faced the daily risk of being **deported**.

As a seventeen-year-old, Angel was afraid to leave his home. He would stick his head out the door and look up and down the street for any sign of immigration officers—and then run as fast as he could to the shop on the corner, buy the eggs his mother needed, and then run home again.

"Avoiding immigration is like playing the lottery," Angel says today. "It's playing the odds that you won't get caught. In exchange, you get the chance to work and make more money in the United States." There are certain things undocumented immigrants do to improve their odds, Angel says. "We make sure our license plates are new on our cars. We keep our car insurance up to date. We cut our hair and try to look clean. We try to look like we're Americans. We try to fake it." And, says Angel, undocumented immigrants pray a lot. " 'Please, Lord,' we say every day, 'don't let that cop behind me stop me!' "

In 1986, Angel's family applied for **amnesty**, and three years later they received permanent residency cards. Finally, they could leave their home and breathe easy. But they were not yet citizens, though they wanted to be.

Meanwhile, Angel was working hard to support his mother, brothers, and grandfather. He graduated from high school, but he couldn't go on to college yet. He didn't have the papers he needed to become a citizen, and the jobs he could get without those papers didn't pay enough for him to save the money he needed for college.

Then in 2006, Angel started working for a church in Phoenix. He became an American citizen at last—and he also became a pastor. Now he works to help other Hispanics, on both sides of the U.S.-Mexican border.

"A border is just a line," he says. "People are people on both sides. They have the same needs. But it's fear that convinces people it's okay to hate each other because of imaginary lines. What it comes down to? It's prejudice."

Angel's job is to do what he can to fight that prejudice—and to protect Latinos from prejudice whenever he can.

One day recently he got a phone call from a young man named Javier. Javier walks with a limp, and he has mental challenges as well. In addition to the prejudice he faces as a Hispanic, he also struggles with the prejudice many people feel toward those with physical and intellectual disabilities. Today, Javier is **indigent**, but he still has one good friend who has stuck by him all his life, a young man his age named Daniel who has always treated him with dignity and respect.

"Pastor, they have Daniel!" Javier told Angel now. He was in tears.

The police had picked up Daniel, an all-too-common story that Angel hears from the people he serves in Phoenix. Angel went immediately to the police station.

"Officer, may I know why you approached this young man?" he asked.

"It doesn't matter!" the police officer replied. "Maybe his brake light didn't work. But now we know he's an illegal."

"Officer, is that justice?" Angel asked.

The police officer looked away. "Go preach to your church, Pastor," he muttered. "I'm not interested."

Daniel was put in jail. His insurance and driving license were invalidated. And then he was deported to Mexico. As a result, he could not get back across the border for his court appearance, and he was fined the full penalty for a broken brake light that he didn't have. And Javier lost his only friend.

Pastor Campos has many stories like this to tell. He also tells of an elderly couple who attend his church. They have lived and worked in the United States for more than twenty years. Each year taxes were deducted from the paychecks for Social Security. But after all these years, they are still undocumented immigrants. They cannot collect any retirement, even though they paid into the system for many years. They are not eligible for Medicare benefits. They face old age with only their savings to pay their living and medical expenses until they die.

Angel Campos' sense of humor, kindness, and faith make him a strong opponent against prejudice.

"Prejudice looks at that couple and says they deserve what they get. Prejudice says they're not Americans and we don't owe them anything." Pastor Campos shakes his head. "And I want to answer, 'Those people helped pay for your food stamps. You're going to retire on their money.' Because there are thousands just like them."

But then, in spite of his anger, he laughs. "And that's one more reason why so many Hispanics are people of faith. If you can't get health insurance, then you pray that much more. You count on God to take care of you."

Recently, a local businessman came to the church where Pastor Campos works. "Will you help us keep illegals out of our neighborhood?" the man asked the church leaders. "Report any that come around? Maybe put up a fence around your property so people can't hang around your buildings when you're not here?"

"We told him we weren't interested." Angel Campos smiles and shakes his head. "Prejudice likes fences—but we like bridges around here. Bridges and doors. Things that help people get somewhere new. That's what we want to build. We're not interested in helping to put up any more fences."

Fighting Prejudice

Not so long ago, Angel Campos was standing in line at his bank, waiting for his turn with the teller. "A guy in line with me started saying offensive stuff, racist stuff. His voice kept getting louder. Most everybody else around me was Anglo. Nobody else was saying anything. I felt like I was surrounded by hate, like everyone in that bank agreed with what the guy was saying."

But then the whole situation changed. An elderly woman spoke up. "Son, you make me embarrassed to be white."

"Everyone in the bank clapped," Angel remembers. "And I realized I'd been wrong. I hadn't been surrounded by prejudice after all."

Sometimes that's all it takes, Angel says: one person to speak out and stand up for what's right.

"And then you have to transform the hatred," he adds. "Change the dynamics. Suddenly, that day in the bank, it was no longer the whites against the Hispanics. It was everyone against the jerk! I could have gotten mad and yelled something back at that guy. But now I could say to him, 'I refuse to hate you.' My job is to be a healer. To help calm the violence and heal the hurt."

Prejudice can all too easily turn into a two-way street, Pastor Campos points out. I hate you, so you hate me. I'm afraid of you, so I try to protect myself against you—and you become afraid of me, so you go on the defensive. The situation can all too easily escalate.

Pastor Campos tell of another incident when he was driving along the highway and came across an RV that was broken down on the side of the road. Stickers with racist slogans were pasted all over the RV. "My job is to be blind to stuff like that," Pastor Campos says. "I can't pay attention to those stickers. So I pull over. Turns out it's an elderly white couple. I fix their problem with the RV. I give them a drink from the cooler in my car. They say thank you, and I'm on my way. Maybe I just did something to help fight prejudice. That's what we have to do, every chance we get. Reach out our hands. Get past the imaginary lines."

Meanwhile, Nicole González Patterson is also doing her part to fight prejudice against Hispanics. But while Angel Campos

Nicole Patterson explains the importance of civic engagement in the battle against prejudice.

Latinos have always been a part of America. They help make America strong.

works for change in one person at a time, Nicole looks at the bigger picture, at the systems that support prejudice and allow it to grow.

The organization where Nicole worked, the Arizona Latino Research Enterprise, wants to help the Hispanic population use their political power. It organizes town-hall events with speakers, and it also makes opportunities for people on both sides of the issues to communicate with each other. The Arizona Latino Research Enterprise is bipartisan; in other words, it doesn't take sides. Instead, it works to create a safe place where people can communicate without fear.

"The hurt is on both sides," Nicole says. "It affects everyone. We need to take prejudice personally, not ignore it. We need to realize how deeply it affects us all."

The first step, says Nicole, is to be honest and pay attention. "We need to recognize prejudice when we see it—and then not try to rationalize it or justify it. People say things like, 'I don't hate Latinos. I just don't want people to break the law.' Or, 'I have nothing against Latino culture. I just think Americans should protect their own culture.' But it's really prejudice. We need to call it what it is. We need to give it a name."

The Arizona Latino Research Enterprise is all about civic engagement, about teaching Hispanics to use their power as

Fighting Prejudice Inside You

We all have some degree of prejudice inside us. Instead of denying it, we need to recognize it in ourselves—and then change. Here are some ways experts suggest you can fight prejudice when you find it inside yourself:

- Learn more about groups of people who are different from you. Read books about their history; read fiction that allows you to walk in their shoes in your imagination; watch movies that portray them accurately.
- Get to know people who are different from you. Practice being a good listener, focusing on what they have to say rather than on your own opinions and experiences. Ask about others' backgrounds and family stories.
- Practice compassion. Imagine what it would feel like to be someone who is different from you. Your imagination is a powerful tool you can use to make the world better!
- Be aware of the words you use. Avoid remarks that are based on stereotypes and challenge those made by others.

- Speak out against jokes and slurs that target people or groups. It is not enough to refuse to laugh; silence sends a message that you are in agreement.
- Volunteer to work with agencies that fight prejudice or that work on behalf of minorities in your community.
- Write letters to your newspaper, speaking out against discrimination in your community.
- Attend local cultural events.
- Eat at ethnic restaurants. Talk to the owners and staff while you're there.
- Believe in yourself. Surprisingly, a lot of the time, psychologists say, prejudice is caused by having a bad self-concept. If you don't like who you are and you don't believe in your own abilities, you're more likely to be scared and threatened by others. People who are comfortable with themselves are also more comfortable with people who are different from themselves.

a community to change the laws. "For kids," says Nicole, "that could be as simple as communicating within the most basic community structures—their families and friends. It means

Prejudice Starts Inside

Sociologists have found that people who are prejudiced toward one group of people also tend to be prejudiced toward other groups. In a study done in 1946, people were asked about their attitudes concerning a variety of ethnic groups, including Danireans, Pirraneans, and Wallonians. The study found that people who were prejudiced toward blacks and Jews also distrusted these other three groups. The catch is that Danireans, Pirraneans, and Wallonians didn't exist! This suggests that prejudice's existence may be rooted within the person who feels prejudice rather than in the group that is feared and hated.

talking to your parents, to your peers, speaking out against prejudice wherever you see it happening."

How do we fight prejudice? "Recognize the power of conversations," Nicole says. "Make connections with other people. You have power to change the way others think. Use your power!"

The church where Angel Campos works is not interested in erecting walls. Instead, it works to deepen and protect the connections between people.

Pastor Angel Campos is a good role model. He is someone who puts his beliefs into action.

"Don't expect someone else to fight prejudice for you," is what Angel Campos says. "It's not the church's job or the school's job or the government's job. It's your job. It's my job. We each got to take responsibility."

Ultimately, Nicole's and Angel's jobs aren't so different. Both of them are working hard to build bridges and open doors.

Prejudice puts up walls. It makes it hard to talk to others or understand them. And those walls can lead to hatred, violence, and even wars.

So do what you can to open doors in the walls made by prejudice. Build bridges that cross the walls.

It's up to you!

FIND OUT MORE

In Books

Cruz, Bárbara C. *Triumphs and Struggles for Latino Civil Rights.* Berkeley Heights, New Jersey: Enslow Publishers, 2008.

Hunter, Miranda. *The Story of Latino Civil Rights: Fighting for Justice.* Broomall, Penn.: Mason Crest Publishers, 2006.

McIntosh, Kenneth. *Latinos Today: Facts and Figures.* Broomall, Penn.: Mason Crest Publishers, 2006.

On the Internet

EVENTS IN HISPANIC AMERICAN HISTORY
www.gale.cengage.com/free_resources/chh/timeline/

LATINO HISTORY PROJECT
museumca.org/LHP/

LATINOS IN HISTORY
teacher.scholastic.com/activities/hispanic/history.htm

PREJUDICE
www.cyh.com/HealthTopics/HealthTopicDetailsKids.
aspx?p=335&np=286&id=2348

GLOSSARY

amnesty: Giving someone a pardon for a crime.

compatible: Able to exist together without conflict.

deported: Forced to leave a country.

economics: The study of wealth and money.

effeminate: Overly feminine, usually used as an insult against males.

exiled: Forced to leave and never return.

indigent: Extremely poor and in need.

limbo: In between two places or situations.

oversimplification: Making something complicated too simple.

phenomenon: A remarkable occurrence.

reconciled: Talking or meeting again in a friendly way after a period of hostility.

sociologists: People who study the way that humans behave.

stigma: A mark of disgrace.

undocumented: Not having the papers that allow one to legally be in a country.

INDEX

BIBLIOGRAPHY

Campos, Angel. Personal communication, January 21, 2011.

Farley, John E. *Majority-Minority Relations*, 5th ed. Upper Saddle River, N.J.: Prentice Hall, 2005.

González, Juan. *Harvest of Empire: A History of Latinos in America*. New York: Penguin, 2011.

Graham, Carol. "Does Inequality Matter to Individual Welfare?" Brookings Institute, January 2005. www.brookings.edu/reports/2005/01poverty_graham.aspx

Henslin, James. *Essentials of Sociology*, 6th ed. Boston: Allyn and Bacon, 2006.

"Immigration Issues." Public Agenda for Citizens. www.publicagenda.org/citizen/issueguides/immigration

Passel, Jeffrey. "Size and Characteristics of the Unauthorized Migrant Population in the U.S." Pew Research Center, March 7, 2006. www.pewhispanic.org/2006/03/07/size-and-characteristics-of-the-unauthorized-migrant-population-in-the-us/

Patterson, Nicole González. Arizona Latino Research Enterprise. Personal communication, January 21, 2011.

PICTURE CREDITS

ABOUT THE AUTHOR

Ellyn Sanna is the author of hundreds of books for children, young adults, and adults. She has also worked for many years as an editor and small-business owner.